CONTENTS

Written by Stevie Derrick

Collins

1 WHAT IS SLIME?

What's gooey and sticky? Slime! Slime – also called mucus – is found naturally in the human body. Mucus is made of mostly water. It acts like a barrier, protecting your body from harmful germs that could make you sick.

There's mucus in your nose, throat, eyes and ears. It surrounds every **organ** in your body.

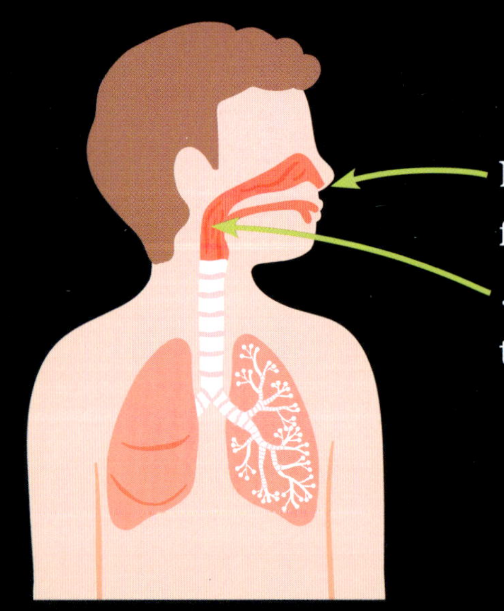

Mucus dribbles down from your nose …

… and oozes from the back of your throat.

You swallow about two litres of it every day!

Humans need slime to stay healthy, but we're not the only ones. Animals produce slime, too.

2 SLIME ON THE MOVE

You've spotted a slime trail in your garden. What animals leave goo behind like this when they move?

Snails and slugs cover their bodies in liquid goo to help them glide along the ground. When they aren't moving, the slime acts like a glue, sticking them to surfaces.

garden snail

leopard slug

SLIME SECRETS

Giant African land snails are about the size of an adult's hand! In hot weather, they can seal themselves inside their shells, using slime to stop from drying out.

SLIME SECRETS

Australian red triangle slugs ooze a special, super-sticky slime when attacked by **predators** like frogs. The slime can glue frogs to trees for days.

3 MONSTER SLIME MAKERS

The creature that made this goo might be the slimiest animal on the planet.

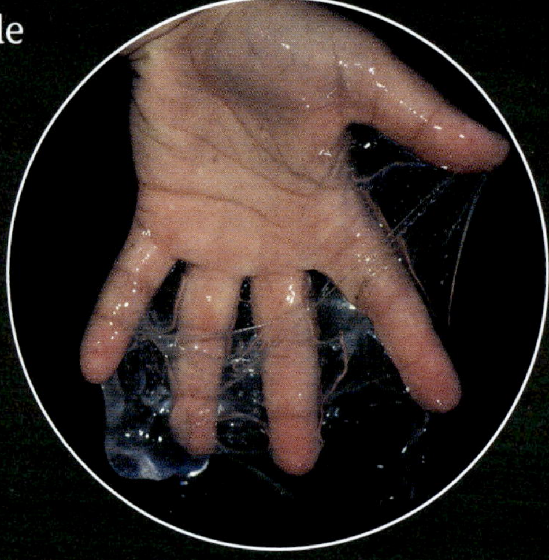

It's a hagfish! When scared, hagfish release less than a teaspoon of mucus. When the slime mixes with seawater, it expands.

Any predators close by will be choked by this gooey liquid, which gives the hagfish time to escape.

SLIME SECRETS

Hagfish tie themselves into a knot and move the knot up and down to scrape slime off their bodies.

This is sea snot. It's a thick, sticky slime that grows underwater. It covers coastlines and harms sea life.

When tiny **organisms** called algae die, they release a sticky slime. This traps things like dead animals and poo in the sea and grows into sea snot.

algae seen under a **microscope**

4 SLIME STEALERS

Some insects love slurping up sap, but these ants steal slime from other bugs. Who do they steal it from?

Slime from these bugs makes leaves shiny.

Aphids are tiny, green bugs that make a sweet slime called honeydew. Some types of ants steal this slime by tickling the aphids until they release it.

The ants herd the aphids, keeping them together and protecting them from predators.

The ants tickle the aphids to milk them of the honeydew.

The aphids release the honeydew, and the ants get a tasty snack.

5 SLIMY TRAPS

These bugs use their glowing bottoms to attract flying insects!

New Zealand glow-worms live in dark caves where they build slimy tubes on the ceiling. From the tubes, they hang sticky threads of silk to trap flying insects.

The sea is full of slime, and some sea creatures use this slime to catch food. This creature launches a mucus net. It's up to two metres long – about the height of a door.

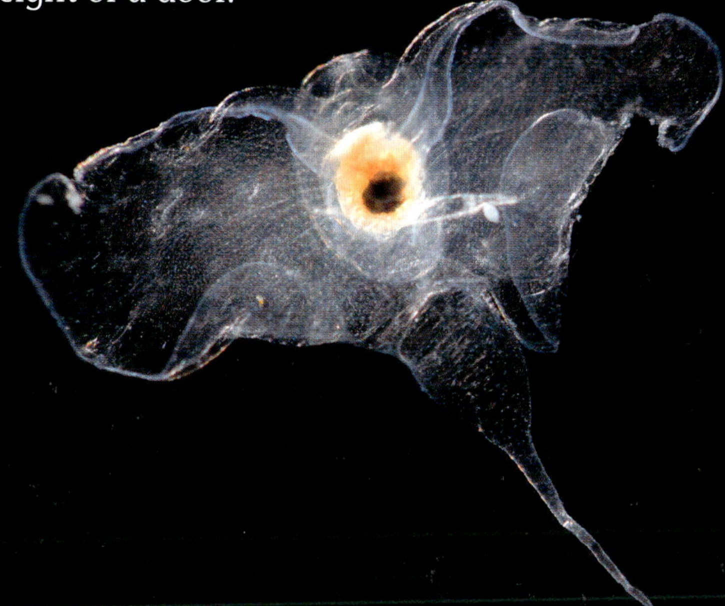

The mucus nets are made by sea snails!

6 SLIME BUBBLES

This colourful sea creature sleeps in a snot bubble.

First, the parrotfish finds a nice spot to sleep.

Then, it blows a slimy bubble from its gills that wraps around it like a sleeping bag.

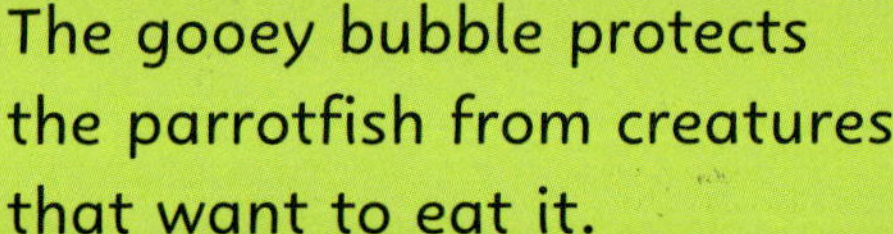

The gooey bubble protects the parrotfish from creatures that want to eat it.

This creature makes a raft from mucus that traps air bubbles.

It's another snail! The slimy raft keeps violet sea snails afloat.

7 DEADLY SLIME

Deadly slime fires from either side of this creature's head!

Velvet worms can shoot out jets of slime from up to 60 cm away. It hardens around their **prey** like glue.

Don't mess with these creatures. They ooze a poisonous slime from their bottom.

If birds or snakes try to eat red-cheeked salamanders, they're in for a nasty surprise!

common garter snake

American robin

8 SLIME PROTECTION

These heavy land animals squeeze a pink sludge all over their body. The slime protects them from the sun. What are they?

They're hippos! Hippos live in hot countries. To protect themselves from the sun's rays, they sweat out two types of slime: the orange acts like sun cream, while the red protects them from harmful bugs that could make them sick.

SLIME SECRETS

When mixed together, the slime makes hippos look pink.

9 SLIMY SNEEZES

Every few minutes, these reptiles sneeze out a mixture of salt and snot.

This sneezy trick allows marine iguanas to get rid of all the saltwater they gulp down when they eat their favourite food: red and green algae.

red and green algae

These sea creatures don't have a nose, but they need to remove mucus from their body in a sneeze-like way.

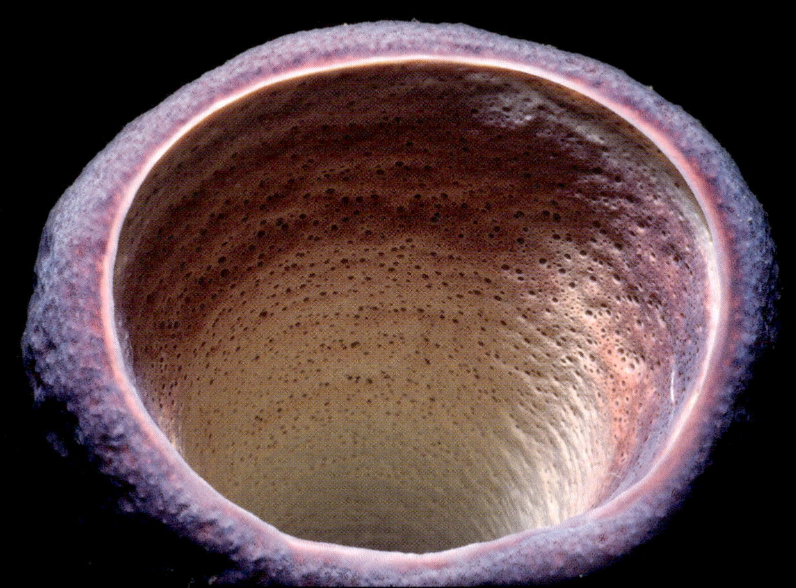

Mucus moves out of sea sponges through tubes. When the mucus reaches the top, sea sponges push it out quickly. The entire "sneeze" takes about 30 minutes.

10 WE ALL NEED SLIME!

While slime might seem sticky and gross, you wouldn't want to be without it.

It stops germs getting into your body and making you sick.

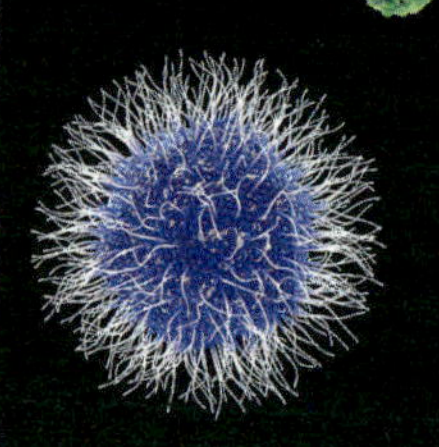

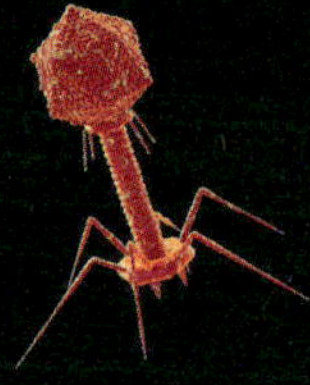

It helps animals slide across the ground.

It protects creatures from predators … and the sun.

The next time you sneeze, remember how useful slime is!

GLOSSARY

microscope something that makes very small things look bigger

organ something that performs a specific function

organisms living things, such as plants or animals

predators animals that hunt other animals

prey an animal that is hunted by other animals

INDEX

WHO LEFT THE SLIME?

Ideas for reading

Written by Gill Matthews
Primary Literacy Consultant

Reading objectives:

- be introduced to non-fiction books that are structured in different ways
- discuss and clarify the meanings of words, linking new meanings to known vocabulary
- draw on what they already know or on background information and vocabulary provided by the teacher
- check that the text makes sense to them as they read and correct inaccurate reading
- answer and ask questions

Spoken language objectives:

- ask relevant questions to extend their understanding and knowledge
- use relevant strategies to build their vocabulary
- use spoken language to develop understanding through speculating, hypothesising, imagining and exploring ideas

Curriculum links: Science: animals, including humans

Word count: 920

Interest words: barrier, protecting, harmful, surrounds, produce

Build a context for reading

- Ask children to look at the front cover and to read the title. Ask them to describe slime.
- Encourage children to predict what the book might be about.
- Read the back-cover blurb. Ask children what they think they are going to find out from the book.
- Point out that this is an information book. Explore children's knowledge and experience of non-fiction. Ask what features they think this book might have.
- Ask children to find the contents page. Discuss the purpose and organisation of a contents list.
- Ask children to find the chapter called *What is slime?*